UNLOCKING THE POWER

BUILDING ELEGANT APPLICATIONS

OLIVER LUCAS JR

TABLE OF CONTENTS

PREFACE

Welcome to the world of Ruby on Rails, a powerful and elegant framework that has revolutionized web development. This book is your comprehensive guide to mastering this framework and building robust, scalable, and maintainable web applications.

Whether you're a seasoned developer or just starting your journey, this book is designed to equip you with the knowledge and skills you need to succeed. We'll delve into the core concepts of Ruby on Rails, from its fundamental principles to advanced techniques.

What You'll Learn:

Ruby Basics: Grasp the fundamentals of the Ruby programming language, including syntax, data structures, and object-oriented programming.

Rails Foundations: Understand the Model-View-Controller (MVC) architecture and how it's implemented in Rails.

Building Web Applications: Learn to create dynamic web applications with Rails, including routing, controllers, and views.

Database Interactions: Master database interactions using ActiveRecord, from basic queries to complex relationships.

Testing Your Applications: Write effective tests to ensure code quality and maintainability.

Deployment Strategies: Deploy your Rails applications to production environments, including Heroku and AWS.

Advanced Topics: Explore advanced concepts like performance optimization, security best practices, and real-world application development.

This book is more than just a reference guide; it's a practical companion that will help you build real-world applications. Each chapter is packed with clear explanations, code examples, and hands-on exercises to reinforce your learning.

So, let's embark on this exciting journey together and unlock the full potential of Ruby on Rails.

Chapter 1

Introduction to Ruby

1.1 What is Ruby?

Ruby is a versatile and powerful programming language known for its elegant syntax and emphasis on programmer productivity. It was created in the mid-1990s by Yukihiro "Matz" Matsumoto with the goal of combining the best aspects of other programming languages like Perl, Smalltalk, and Python.

Key Characteristics of Ruby:

Object-Oriented: Everything in Ruby is an object, including primitive data types. This allows for a consistent and intuitive programming style.

Dynamically Typed: You don't need to declare variable types explicitly, making code more concise and flexible.

Interpreted: Ruby code is executed line by line, which can be helpful for rapid development and debugging.

High-Level Syntax: Ruby's syntax is designed to be human-readable and easy to learn. It often resembles natural language, making it a great choice for beginners.

Rich Standard Library: Ruby comes with a comprehensive standard library that provides a wide range of functionalities, reducing the need for external libraries.

Active Community: A large and active community of developers contributes to Ruby's ecosystem, providing support, libraries, and frameworks.

Common Uses of Ruby:

Web Development: Ruby on Rails, a popular web framework built on Ruby, is widely used for building web applications. It offers a rapid development approach and a strong emphasis on convention over configuration.

Data Processing and Analysis: Ruby is well-suited for tasks like data mining, data cleaning, and data analysis. Libraries like RSpec and Test::Unit are used for testing and quality assurance.

System Administration: Ruby can be used to automate system administration tasks, such as managing servers, deploying applications, and configuring systems.

DevOps: Ruby is often used for DevOps tasks like configuration management and automation. Tools like Puppet and Chef are built on Ruby.

Game Development: Ruby can be used to create games, especially with the help of frameworks like Gosu and Shoes.

If you're looking for a language that is both powerful and easy to learn, Ruby is an excellent choice. Its elegant syntax, rich ecosystem, and versatility make it a popular choice for developers around the world.

1.2 Why Choose Ruby?

Why Choose Ruby?

Ruby, with its elegant syntax and powerful features, offers several compelling reasons to choose it for your next project:

1. Developer Productivity:

Concise and Readable Syntax: Ruby's syntax is designed to be human-readable, making it easier to write and maintain code.

Rapid Development: Ruby on Rails, a popular web framework built on Ruby, emphasizes convention over configuration, allowing developers to build web applications quickly.

2. Strong Community and Ecosystem:

Active Community: A large and active community of developers provides support, libraries, and frameworks.

Rich Ecosystem: Ruby boasts a vast ecosystem of gems (libraries) that extend its functionality and accelerate development.

3. Object-Oriented Paradigm:

Everything is an Object: Ruby's object-oriented nature promotes code reusability and modularity.

Inheritance and Polymorphism: Powerful object-oriented concepts enable flexible and scalable designs.

4. Flexibility and Expressiveness:

Metaprogramming: Ruby's metaprogramming capabilities allow developers to modify the language itself, enabling powerful and elegant solutions.

Domain-Specific Languages (DSLs): Create custom languages tailored to specific problem domains, enhancing code readability and maintainability.

5. Testing and Quality Assurance:

Robust Testing Framework: Ruby's built-in testing framework, RSpec, facilitates writing comprehensive and maintainable tests.

Test-Driven Development (TDD): Encourages writing tests before code, leading to higher quality and more reliable software.

6. Scalability and Performance:

Scalable Architectures: Ruby on Rails can handle high traffic loads and complex applications with proper architecture and optimization techniques.

Performance Optimization: Techniques like caching, database optimization, and asynchronous processing can improve performance.

7. Job Market and Career Opportunities:

High Demand: Ruby developers are in demand, especially for web development and startups.

Well-Paying Jobs: Ruby positions often come with competitive salaries.

8. Fun and Enjoyable:

Developer Happiness: Ruby's elegant syntax and focus on developer productivity make it a joy to work with.

1.3 Setting Up Your Ruby Environment

To start your Ruby programming journey, you'll need to set up a suitable development environment. Here's a general guide:

1. Installing Ruby:

Using a Package Manager:

For macOS:

Bash

```
xcode-select --install
brew install ruby
```

For Linux (Ubuntu, Debian):

Bash

```
sudo apt update
sudo apt install ruby-full
```

For Windows:

Using RubyInstaller: Download the installer from the official Ruby website and follow the instructions.

2. Verifying Installation: Open your terminal or command prompt and type:

Bash

```
ruby -v
```

This should display the installed Ruby version.

3. Installing a Text Editor or IDE: A good text editor or IDE can significantly enhance your development experience. Popular choices include:

Text Editors:

Visual Studio Code: A versatile and customizable code editor.

Sublime Text: A powerful and fast text editor.

Atom: A highly customizable and open-source text editor.

Integrated Development Environments (IDEs):

RubyMine: A powerful IDE specifically designed for Ruby and Rails development.

4. Setting Up a Version Control System (Optional): A version control system like Git helps you track changes to your code and collaborate with others. You can install Git using your package manager or by downloading it from the official Git website.

5. Installing a Package Manager (Optional): A package manager like `Bundler` helps manage dependencies for your Ruby projects. Install it using:

Bash

```
gem install bundler
```

Additional Tips:

Keep Your Ruby Version Up-to-Date: Regularly update Ruby to benefit from the latest features and security fixes.

Use a Good Text Editor or IDE: A good development environment can significantly improve your productivity.

Learn Basic Terminal Commands: Basic terminal commands are essential for navigating your file system, running Ruby scripts, and managing packages.

Practice Regularly: The more you practice, the better you'll become.

By following these steps, you'll have a solid foundation to start your Ruby programming journey. Would you like to dive deeper into a specific topic, such as writing your first Ruby program or using a particular framework like Ruby on Rails?

Chapter 2

Ruby Basics

2.1 Variables and Data Types

Variables

In Ruby, variables are used to store values. They are dynamically typed, meaning you don't need to declare their data type explicitly. To assign a value to a variable, you use the assignment operator (=).

Example:

Ruby

```
name = "Alice"
age = 30
is_student = true
```

Data Types

Ruby supports various data types, including:

1. Numbers:

Integers: Whole numbers like 1, -10, 1000.

Floating-Point Numbers: Numbers with decimal points like 3.14, -2.5.

2. Strings: Sequences of characters enclosed in single or double quotes.

Ruby

```ruby
greeting = "Hello, world!"
```

3. Symbols: Unique identifiers often used as keys in hashes.

Ruby

```ruby
color = :blue
```

4. Booleans: Represents truth values, either `true` or `false`.

Ruby

```ruby
is_raining = false
```

5. Arrays: Ordered collections of objects.

Ruby

```ruby
fruits = ["apple", "banana", "cherry"]
```

6. Hashes: Unordered collections of key-value pairs.

Ruby

```ruby
person = { name: "Bob", age: 25, city: "New York" }
```

Basic Operations

Ruby supports basic arithmetic operations:

Ruby

```ruby
# Addition
result = 5 + 3

# Subtraction
result = 10 - 4

# Multiplication
result = 2 * 6

# Division
result = 15 / 3

# Modulus (remainder)
result = 10 % 3
```

String Concatenation:

Ruby

```ruby
first_name = "John"
last_name = "Doe"
full_name = first_name + " " + last_name
```

String Interpolation:

Ruby

```ruby
name = "Alice"
```

```
age = 30
greeting = "Hello, #{name}. You are #{age} years
old."
```

By understanding these fundamental concepts, you can start building more complex Ruby programs. Would you like to delve deeper into a specific topic or practice with some exercises?

2.2 Operators in Ruby

Operators are symbols that perform specific operations on operands. Ruby supports various types of operators:

Arithmetic Operators

These operators perform basic arithmetic operations:

Operator	Description	Example
+	Addition	5 + 3
-	Subtraction	10 - 4
*	Multiplication	2 * 6
/	Division	15 / 3
%	Modulus (remainder)	10 % 3
**	Exponentiation	2 ** 3

Comparison Operators

These operators compare values and return a boolean result:

Operator	Description	Example
==	Equal to	5 == 5
!=	Not equal to	3 != 4
>	Greater than	10 > 5
<	Less than	2 < 7
>=	Greater than or equal to	5 >= 5
<=	Less than or equal to	3 <= 4

Logical Operators

These operators combine boolean expressions:

Operator	Description	Example
&&	Logical AND	(5 > 3) && (2 < 4)
	Logical OR	
!	Logical NOT	! (5 > 3)

Assignment Operators

These operators assign values to variables:

Operator	Description	Example
=	Assignment	x = 5
+=	Add and assign	x += 3
-=	Subtract and assign	x -= 2
*=	Multiply and assign	x *= 4
/=	Divide and assign	x /= 2
%=	Modulus and assign	x %= 3
**=	Exponentiation and assign	x **= 2

Bitwise Operators

These operators perform bitwise operations on integers:

Operator	Description	Example
&	Bitwise AND	5 & 3
		Bitwise OR	
^	Bitwise XOR	5 ^ 3
~	Bitwise NOT	~5

<<	Left shift	`5 << 2`
>>	Right shift	`5 >> 1`

Remember that the order of operations follows the standard mathematical rules: parentheses, exponents, multiplication and division, addition and subtraction. You can use parentheses to group expressions and control the order of evaluation.

Would you like to practice with some examples or explore a specific operator in more detail?

2.3 Control Flow in Ruby

Control flow statements allow you to control the execution flow of your Ruby programs. Here are some of the most common control flow structures:

Conditional Statements

1. if Statement

Ruby

```ruby
if condition
  # code to execute if condition is true
end
```

2. if-else Statement

Ruby

```ruby
if condition
  # code to execute if condition is true
else
```

```
  # code to execute if condition is false
end
```

3. `if-elsif-else` Statement

Ruby

```ruby
if condition1
  # code to execute if condition1 is true
elsif condition2
  # code to execute if condition1 is false and
condition2 is true
else
  # code to execute if both conditions are false
end
```

Loops

1. `while` Loop

Ruby

```ruby
while condition
  # code to execute while condition is true
end
```

2. `until` Loop

Ruby

```ruby
until condition
  # code to execute until condition is true
```

```
end
```

3. for **Loop**

Ruby

```ruby
for element in array
  # code to execute for each element in the array
end
```

4. each **Method**

Ruby

```ruby
array.each do |element|
  # code to execute for each element in the array
end
```

Example:

Ruby

```ruby
age = 25

if age >= 18
  puts "You are an adult."
else
  puts "You are a minor."
end

numbers = [1, 2, 3, 4, 5]
```

```
numbers.each do |number|
  puts number * 2
end
```

Key Points:

Indentation is crucial in Ruby to define code blocks.

The `end` keyword marks the end of a block.

Use `break` to exit a loop prematurely.

Use `next` to skip to the next iteration of a loop.

By understanding these control flow structures, you can create more dynamic and responsive Ruby programs. Would you like to practice with some exercises or explore more advanced control flow techniques?

2.4 Methods and Functions

Methods and Functions in Ruby

In Ruby, methods are blocks of code that perform specific tasks. They are defined using the `def` keyword and can take parameters and return values.

Defining a Method:

Ruby

```
def greet(name)
  puts "Hello, #{name}!"
end
```

Calling a Method:

Ruby

```ruby
greet("Alice")
```

Returning a Value:

Ruby

```ruby
def square(number)
  return number * number
end

result = square(5)
puts result
```

Default Arguments:

Ruby

```ruby
def greet(name = "World")
  puts "Hello, #{name}!"
end

greet()  # Output: Hello, World!
greet("Alice")  # Output: Hello, Alice!
```

Variable Number of Arguments:

Ruby

```ruby
def sum(*numbers)
  total = 0
  numbers.each { |number| total += number }
  return total
end

result = sum(1, 2, 3, 4, 5)
puts result
```

Keyword Arguments:

Ruby

```ruby
def greet(name:, age:)
    puts "Hello, #{name}! You are #{age} years
old."
end

greet(name: "Bob", age: 30)
```

Blocks and Lambdas:

Blocks are anonymous code blocks that can be passed to methods as arguments. Lambdas are similar to blocks but can be assigned to variables.

Ruby

```ruby
def calculate(number, &block)
  result = block.call(number)
  puts result
end
```

```ruby
calculate(5) { |x| x * 2 }
```

Methods as Objects:

In Ruby, methods are first-class objects, meaning they can be assigned to variables, passed as arguments, and returned from other methods.

Ruby

```ruby
greeting_method = method(:greet)
greeting_method.call("Bob")
```

By understanding methods and functions, you can create well-organized, reusable, and efficient Ruby code. Would you like to practice with some exercises or explore a specific aspect of methods and functions in more detail?

Chapter 3

Object-Oriented Programming with Ruby

3.1 Classes and Objects

Classes and Objects: The Building Blocks of Object-Oriented Programming

In Ruby, object-oriented programming (OOP) is a fundamental paradigm that revolves around the concept of classes and objects.

Classes

A class is a blueprint or template for creating objects. It defines the properties (attributes) and behaviors (methods) that objects of that class will[1] have.

Example:

Ruby

```ruby
class Dog
  attr_accessor :name, :breed, :age

  def initialize(name, breed, age)
    @name = name
    @breed = breed
    @age = age
  end

  def bark
    puts "Woof!"
```

```
    end
end
```

In this example, `Dog` is a class that defines the attributes `name`, `breed`, and `age`, as well as the `bark` method.

Objects

An object is an instance of a class. It represents a real-world entity with specific properties and behaviors.

Example:

Ruby

```
fido = Dog.new("Fido", "Golden Retriever", 3)
```

Here, `fido` is an object of the `Dog` class. It has the attributes `name`, `breed`, and `age`, and can perform the `bark` method.

Key Concepts in OOP:

Encapsulation: Wrapping data and methods within a class to protect data integrity and control access.

Inheritance: Creating new classes (child classes) that inherit properties and methods from existing classes (parent classes).

Polymorphism: The ability of objects of different classes to respond to the same method call in different ways.

By understanding classes and objects, you can create well-structured, modular, and reusable Ruby code.

3.2 Inheritance and Polymorphism

Inheritance is a fundamental concept in object-oriented programming (OOP) that allows you to create new classes[1] (child classes or subclasses) that inherit the properties and methods of existing classes (parent classes or superclasses). This promotes code reusability and helps to organize complex hierarchies of classes.

Example:

Ruby

```ruby
class Animal
  def initialize(name)
    @name = name
  end

  def eat
    puts "#{@name} is eating."
  end
end

class Dog < Animal
  def bark
    puts "#{@name} is barking."
  end
end

fido = Dog.new("Fido")
fido.eat # Output: Fido is eating.
fido.bark # Output: Fido is barking.
```

In this example, the `Dog` class inherits from the `Animal` class. It inherits the `initialize` and `eat` methods from the parent class and adds its own specific behavior, the `bark` method.

Polymorphism

Polymorphism is the ability of objects of different classes to respond to the same method call in different ways. This is often achieved through method overriding and method overloading.

Method Overriding

Method overriding occurs when a subclass provides a specific implementation[2] of a method that is already defined[3] in its parent class.

Example:

Ruby

```ruby
class Vehicle
  def move
    puts "Vehicle is moving."
  end
end

class Car < Vehicle
  def move
    puts "Car is driving."
  end
end

class Bicycle < Vehicle
  def move
    puts "Bicycle is pedaling."
  end
```

```
end

car = Car.new
bicycle = Bicycle.new

car.move # Output: Car is driving.
bicycle.move # Output: Bicycle is pedaling.
```

Method Overloading

Method overloading is not directly supported in Ruby. However, you can achieve similar behavior using default arguments or variable-length argument lists.

By understanding inheritance and polymorphism, you can create flexible and extensible object-oriented designs in Ruby.

3.3 Modules and Mixins

Modules

Modules are a way to group methods and constants together in Ruby. They can be included in classes to provide additional functionality. Modules cannot be instantiated as objects.

Example:

Ruby

```
module Swimmable
  def swim
    puts "I can swim!"
  end
end
```

```ruby
class Duck
  include Swimmable
end

duck = Duck.new
duck.swim # Output: I can swim!
```

Mixins

Mixins are a way to include the methods of one module into another module or class. They are similar to multiple inheritance, but they avoid the complexities associated with it.

Example:

Ruby

```ruby
module Flyable
  def fly
    puts "I can fly!"
  end
end

class Bird
  include Flyable, Swimmable
end

bird = Bird.new
bird.fly # Output: I can fly!
bird.swim # Output: I can swim!
```

Key Points:

Modules cannot be instantiated.

Modules can be included in multiple classes.

Mixins allow you to share code between different classes.

Modules can also be used to define namespaces.

By understanding modules and mixins, you can create well-organized and reusable code in Ruby.

3.4 Encapsulation

Encapsulation is a fundamental concept in object-oriented programming (OOP) that involves bundling data (attributes) and methods[1] (behaviors) that operate on that data within a single unit, the class. This encapsulation helps to protect the data from accidental modification and provides a controlled interface for accessing and manipulating the data.

Key Benefits of Encapsulation:

Data Hiding: Encapsulation hides the internal implementation details of a class, making the code more modular and easier to maintain.

Modularity: Encapsulation promotes modularity by breaking down complex systems into smaller, self-contained units.

Code Reusability: Encapsulated classes can be reused in different parts of the application or even in different projects.

Security: Encapsulation helps to protect sensitive data by restricting access to it through well-defined methods.

Example:

Ruby

```ruby
class Person
  attr_accessor :name, :age
```

```ruby
  private
  def initialize(name, age)
    @name = name
    @age = age
  end
end

person = Person.new("Alice", 30)
puts person.name # Output: Alice
```

In this example:

The `Person` class encapsulates the `name` and `age` attributes.

The `initialize` method is private, meaning it can only be accessed within the class itself.

The `attr_accessor` method creates public getter and setter methods for the `name` and `age` attributes.

By using encapsulation, you can create well-structured, maintainable, and secure object-oriented programs in Ruby.

Chapter 4

Working with Data Structures

4.1 Arrays in Ruby

Arrays are ordered collections of objects in Ruby. They are versatile and can store elements of various data types.

Creating an Array:

Ruby

```ruby
# Empty array
empty_array = []

# Array with elements
numbers = [1, 2, 3, 4, 5]
mixed_array = ["apple", 25, true]
```

Accessing Elements:

You can access elements using zero-based indexing:

Ruby

```ruby
first_element = numbers[0]   # Accesses the first
element
last_element = numbers[-1]   # Accesses the last
element
```

Modifying Elements:

Ruby

```ruby
numbers[2] = 10    # Assigns 10 to the third
element
```

Adding Elements:

Appending to the end:

Ruby

```ruby
numbers << 6   # Adds 6 to the end
```

Inserting at a specific index:

Ruby

```ruby
numbers.insert(1, 7)   # Inserts 7 at index 1
```

Removing Elements:

Removing the last element:

Ruby

```ruby
numbers.pop
```

Removing the first element:

Ruby

```ruby
numbers.shift
```

Removing an element at a specific index:

Ruby

```ruby
numbers.delete_at(2)
```

Iterating Over an Array:

Ruby

```ruby
numbers.each do |number|
  puts number
end
```

Common Array Methods:

`length`: Returns the number of elements.

`empty?`: Checks if the array is empty.

`include?`: Checks if an element is present.

`sort`: Sorts the array.

`reverse`: Reverses the order of elements.

`join`: Concatenates elements into a string.

`map`: Creates a new array by transforming each element.

`select`: Creates a new array with elements that meet a certain condition.

Arrays are a fundamental data structure in Ruby, and understanding how to work with them is essential for writing effective Ruby programs.

4.2 Hashes in Ruby

Hashes, also known as dictionaries or associative arrays, are unordered collections of key-value pairs. They are a powerful data structure for storing and retrieving data efficiently.

Creating a Hash:

Ruby

```ruby
person = {
  name: "Alice",
  age: 30,
  city: "New York"
}
```

Accessing Values:

Ruby

```ruby
name = person[:name]   # Accessing the value
associated with the key :name
```

Adding or Modifying Key-Value Pairs:

Ruby

```ruby
person[:occupation] = "Engineer"   # Adds a new
key-value pair
person[:age] = 31   # Modifies the value of an
existing key
```

Iterating Over a Hash:

Ruby

```ruby
person.each do |key, value|
  puts "#{key}: #{value}"
end
```

Common Hash Methods:

`keys`: Returns an array of keys.

`values`: Returns an array of values.

`has_key?`: Checks if a key exists.

`has_value?`: Checks if a value exists.

`delete`: Removes a key-value pair.

`merge`: Merges two hashes.

Example:

Ruby

```ruby
colors = {
  primary: ["red", "blue", "yellow"],
  secondary: ["green", "orange", "purple"]
}

colors[:tertiary] = ["brown", "gray", "black"]

colors.each do |color_type, colors|
  puts "#{color_type}: #{colors.join(', ')}"
end
```

Hashes are a versatile data structure that can be used to represent complex data relationships in Ruby. By understanding how to create, access, and manipulate hashes, you can write more efficient and expressive Ruby code.

4.3 Strings in Ruby

Strings are sequences of characters enclosed in single quotes (') or double quotes ("). They are used to represent textual data.

Creating Strings:

Ruby

```ruby
single_quoted_string = 'Hello, world!'
double_quoted_string = "This is a double-quoted string."
```

Accessing Characters:

You can access individual characters using indexing:

Ruby

```
first_character = single_quoted_string[0]    #
Accesses the first character
last_character = double_quoted_string[-1]    #
Accesses the last character
```

String Concatenation:

You can concatenate strings using the + operator:

Ruby

```
greeting = "Hello"
name = "Alice"
message = greeting + " " + name
```

String Interpolation:

You can embed expressions within double-quoted strings using #{}:

Ruby

```
age = 30
message = "You are #{age} years old."
```

Common String Methods:

`length`: Returns the length of the string.

`upcase`: Converts the string to uppercase.

`downcase`: Converts the string to lowercase.

`capitalize`: Capitalizes the first letter.

`reverse`: Reverses the order of characters.

`split`: Splits the string into an array of substrings.

`join`: Joins elements of an array into a string.

`include?`: Checks if a substring is present.

Example:

Ruby

```ruby
text = "This is a sample string"

puts text.length  # Output: 21
puts  text.upcase   # Output:  THIS  IS  A  SAMPLE
STRING
puts  text.split   # Output:  ["This",  "is",  "a",
"sample", "string"]
```

Strings are fundamental to many programming tasks, and understanding their properties and methods is essential for writing efficient and expressive Ruby code.

4.4 Ranges in Ruby

Ranges represent a sequence of numbers. They are often used in loops, conditional statements, and array slicing.

Creating a Range:

Ruby

```ruby
# Inclusive range (includes both endpoints)
numbers = 1..5

# Exclusive range (excludes the end point)
letters = 'a'..'e'
```

Iterating Over a Range:

Ruby

```ruby
(1..5).each do |number|
  puts number
end
```

Checking Membership:

Ruby

```ruby
puts (1..10).include?(7)  # Output: true
```

Converting a Range to an Array:

Ruby

```ruby
array = (1..5).to_a
```

Common Range Methods:

`first`: Returns the first element.

`last`: Returns the last element.

`min`: Returns the minimum value.

`max`: Returns the maximum value.

Example:

Ruby

```ruby
for number in 1..10
  puts number
end

puts (10..20).to_a
```

Ranges are a concise and powerful way to represent sequences of numbers in Ruby. They can be used to simplify various programming tasks.

Chapter 5

Input/Output Operations

5.1 Reading from Files in Ruby

To read from a file in Ruby, you can use the `File.open` method. This method opens a file and returns a file object. You can then use the `read` method to read the entire contents of the file or the `readlines` method to read the file line by line.

Reading the Entire File:

Ruby

```ruby
file = File.open("file.txt", "r")
contents = file.read
file.close

puts contents
```

Reading Line by Line:

Ruby

```ruby
File.open("file.txt", "r") do |file|
  file.each_line do |line|
    puts line
  end
end
```

Explanation:

Opening the File:

`File.open("file.txt", "r")`: Opens the file named "file.txt" in read mode (`"r"`).

Reading the File:

`file.read`: Reads the entire contents of the file and returns a string.

`file.each_line`: Iterates over each line of the file.

Closing the File:

`file.close`: Closes the file to release system resources.

Best Practices:

Using `File.open` **with a block:** This ensures that the file is automatically closed when the block exits, even if an exception occurs.

Handling Exceptions: Use `begin-rescue-end` blocks to handle potential errors like file not found or permission denied.

Closing the File: Always close the file after you're done with it to avoid resource leaks.

Example with Error Handling:

Ruby

```ruby
begin
  File.open("file.txt", "r") do |file|
    file.each_line do |line|
      puts line
    end
```

```
    end           .
rescue Errno::ENOENT => e
  puts "File not found: #{e.message}"
rescue StandardError => e
  puts "An error occurred: #{e.message}"
end
```

By following these guidelines and using the appropriate methods, you can effectively read data from files in Ruby.

5.2 Writing to Files

Writing to Files in Ruby

To write to a file in Ruby, you can again use the File.open method, but this time you'll open the file in write mode ("w") or append mode ("a").

Writing to a New File:

Ruby

```
File.open("output.txt", "w") do |file|
  file.write("Hello, world!\n")
  file.write("This is a new line.")
end
```

Appending to an Existing File:

Ruby

```
File.open("output.txt", "a") do |file|
  file.write("\nThis is an appended line.")
```

```
end
```

Explanation:

Opening the File:

`File.open("output.txt", "w")`: Opens the file "output.txt" in write mode. If the file doesn't exist, it will be created.

`File.open("output.txt", "a")`: Opens the file "output.txt" in append mode. If the file doesn't exist, it will be created.

Writing to the File:

`file.write`: Writes the specified string to the file.

Closing the File:

The `File.open` block ensures that the file is automatically closed when the block exits.

Best Practices:

Error Handling: Use `begin-rescue-end` blocks to handle potential errors like disk full or permission denied.

File Permissions: Ensure that you have the necessary permissions to write to the file.

Closing the File: Always close the file after you're done with it to avoid resource leaks.

By following these guidelines, you can effectively write data to files in Ruby.

5.3 Command-Line Arguments in Ruby

Command-line arguments are values passed to a Ruby script when it's executed from the command line. These arguments can be used to customize the behavior of the script.

Accessing Command-Line Arguments:

Ruby provides the `ARGV` global variable to access command-line arguments. It's an array containing the arguments passed to the script.

Example:

Ruby

```ruby
# script.rb
puts "Hello, #{ARGV[0]}!"
```

To run this script with an argument:

Bash

```bash
ruby script.rb Alice
```

This will output:

```
Hello, Alice!
```

Iterating Over Arguments:

Ruby

```ruby
ARGV.each do |arg|
  puts arg
end
```

Common Use Cases:

Customizing Script Behavior:

Ruby

```ruby
# script.rb
if ARGV[0] == "help"
  puts "Usage: ruby script.rb <filename>"
else
  # Process the filename
end
```

Passing Configuration Options:

Ruby

```ruby
# script.rb
if ARGV[0] == "--verbose"
  puts "Verbose mode enabled."
end
```

Processing Input Files:

Ruby

```ruby
# script.rb
File.open(ARGV[0], "r") do |file|
  # Process the file
end
```

Key Points:

The first argument is at index 0, the second at index 1, and so on.

You can use `ARGV.length` to get the number of arguments.

For more complex argument parsing, consider using libraries like `optparse`.

By effectively using command-line arguments, you can create more flexible and customizable Ruby scripts.

Chapter 6

Exception Handling

6.1 Understanding Exceptions in Ruby

In Ruby, exceptions are events that occur during the execution of a program that disrupt the normal flow of control. They are used to signal errors, unexpected conditions, or exceptional circumstances.

Types of Exceptions:

Standard Errors: These are general exceptions that can occur in any Ruby program. Examples include `StandardError`, `RuntimeError`, and `ArgumentError`.

System Errors: These are exceptions related to system-level errors, such as file operations or network issues. Examples include `IOError` and `SystemCallError`.

Handling Exceptions:

To handle exceptions in Ruby, we use a `begin-rescue-end` block:

Ruby

```
begin
  # Code that might raise an exception
rescue ExceptionType => e
  # Code to handle the specific exception type
else
  # Code to execute if no exceptions are raised
ensure
```

```
    # Code to always execute, regardless of
exceptions
end
```

Example:

Ruby

```ruby
begin
    File.open("nonexistent_file.txt", "r") do
|file|
    # Process the file
  end
rescue Errno::ENOENT => e
  puts "File not found: #{e.message}"
end
```

Key Points:

The `rescue` block catches specific exception types.

The `else` block executes if no exceptions are raised.

The `ensure` block always executes, regardless of whether an exception is raised.

You can use `raise` to manually raise an exception.

Best Practices:

Use specific exception types to catch and handle different error conditions.

Provide informative error messages to help with debugging.

Use `ensure` blocks to clean up resources, such as closing files or database connections.

Consider using custom exception classes to represent specific error conditions in your application.

By understanding and effectively handling exceptions, you can write more robust and reliable Ruby programs.

6.2 Handling Exceptions with `begin`, `rescue`, and `ensure`

In Ruby, the `begin`, `rescue`, and `ensure` keywords are used to handle exceptions gracefully. This ensures that your program doesn't crash unexpectedly and can recover from errors.

Here's a breakdown of how they work:

1. `begin` **Block:**

Encloses the code that might raise an exception.

2. `rescue` **Block:**

Executes if an exception is raised within the `begin` block.

You can specify the type of exception to catch using `ExceptionType => e`.

The `e` variable will hold the exception object, providing information about the error.

3. `ensure` **Block:**

Executes regardless of whether an exception is raised or not.

Often used for cleanup tasks like closing files or database connections.

Example:

Ruby

```ruby
def divide(x, y)
  begin
    result = x / y
    puts "Result: #{result}"
  rescue ZeroDivisionError => e
    puts "Error: Division by zero: #{e.message}"
  ensure
    puts "This will always execute"
  end
end

divide(10, 0)
```

Explanation:

The `begin` block attempts to divide `x` by `y`.

If a `ZeroDivisionError` is raised, the `rescue` block catches it and prints an error message.

The `ensure` block executes, printing a message regardless of whether an exception occurred.

Key Points:

Use specific exception types in the `rescue` block to handle different error scenarios.

The `ensure` block is ideal for cleanup tasks that must be performed, such as closing files or releasing resources.

You can use `raise` to manually raise an exception.

Consider using custom exception classes to represent specific error conditions in your application.

By effectively using `begin`, `rescue`, and `ensure`, you can create more robust and resilient Ruby applications.

6.3 Raising Custom Exceptions in Ruby

While Ruby provides a rich set of built-in exceptions, you can also define your own custom exceptions to represent specific error conditions in your application. This allows you to create more informative and tailored error messages.

Creating a Custom Exception Class:

Ruby

```ruby
class MyCustomError < StandardError
  # Optional: Add custom attributes or methods
end
```

Raising a Custom Exception:

Ruby

```ruby
raise MyCustomError, "This is a custom error message"
```

Handling a Custom Exception:

Ruby

```ruby
begin
  # Code that might raise the custom exception
```

```ruby
rescue MyCustomError => e
  puts "Caught a custom error: #{e.message}"
end
```

Example:

Ruby

```ruby
class InsufficientFundsError < StandardError
end

def withdraw(amount)
  if balance < amount
      raise InsufficientFundsError, "Insufficient
funds"
  else
    # Withdraw the amount
  end
end
```

Key Points:

Custom exceptions should be derived from `StandardError` or a more specific exception class.

You can add custom attributes to your exception class to provide additional information about the error.

When raising a custom exception, you can provide a message to describe the error.

Use `rescue` blocks to catch and handle custom exceptions.

By creating and raising custom exceptions, you can improve the error handling and debugging capabilities of your Ruby applications.

Chapter 7

Metaprogramming

7.1 Method Missing in Ruby

Method missing is a powerful metaprogramming technique in Ruby that allows you to define a default behavior for methods that don't exist on an object. This can be used to create dynamic and flexible object-oriented designs.

How it Works:

When a method is called on an object, Ruby first checks if the method is defined on the object's class or any of its ancestors.

If the method is not found, Ruby invokes the method_missing method.

You can define the method_missing method in your class to handle undefined method calls.

Basic Example:

Ruby

```ruby
class DynamicObject
  def method_missing(method_name, *args, &block)
    puts "Method '#{method_name}' not found."
  end
end

obj = DynamicObject.new
```

```
obj.non_existent_method        #    Output:    Method
'non_existent_method' not found.
```

More Advanced Usage:

You can use `method_missing` to implement dynamic attribute access, lazy loading, or custom method dispatching:

Ruby

```ruby
class DynamicAttributes
  def method_missing(method_name, *args)
    # Dynamic attribute access
    if method_name.to_s =~ /^(.+)=$/
      instance_variable_set("@#$1", args.first)
    else
      instance_variable_get("@#{method_name}")
    end
  end
end

obj = DynamicAttributes.new
obj.name = "Alice"
puts obj.name
```

Important Considerations:

Use `method_missing` judiciously, as it can make code less predictable and harder to debug.

Consider using other metaprogramming techniques like `define_method` or `send` for more specific scenarios.

Always provide informative error messages when using `method_missing`.

By understanding method missing, you can create more flexible and dynamic Ruby objects. However, it's important to use this technique responsibly and consider the trade-offs in terms of code readability and maintainability.

7.2 Open Classes in Ruby

In Ruby, classes are open, which means you can modify their behavior even after they've been defined. This allows for dynamic extensions and customization of existing classes.

Modifying Existing Classes:

Ruby

```ruby
class String
  def reverse_words
    self.split.reverse.join(" ")
  end
end

puts "hello world".reverse_words # Output: world hello
```

Adding Methods to Built-in Classes:

Ruby

```
class Array
  def my_custom_method
    # Custom method logic
  end
end
```

Key Points:

Open classes provide flexibility and power to extend existing classes.

Use this feature with caution, as it can make code more complex and harder to understand.

Consider using modules to add functionality to multiple classes without modifying the original classes.

When to Use Open Classes:

Adding minor functionality: For small, specific additions to existing classes.

Creating domain-specific languages (DSLs): To extend the language's syntax and semantics.

Monkey patching: A controversial technique to modify existing code at runtime (use with care).

When to Avoid Open Classes:

Modifying core classes: This can lead to unexpected behavior and conflicts with other libraries.

Overriding existing methods: This can break existing code.

By understanding open classes, you can create more flexible and expressive Ruby code. However, it's important to use this feature judiciously and consider the potential impact on code maintainability.

7.3 Monkey Patching

Monkey patching is a technique in Ruby that involves modifying the behavior of existing classes or modules at runtime. It's a powerful tool for customizing and extending functionality, but it should be used with caution.

How it Works:

Identify the Class or Module: Determine the class or module you want to modify.

Reopen the Class or Module: Use the open keyword to reopen the class or module.

Add or Modify Methods: Define new methods or redefine existing ones within the reopened class or module.

Example:

Ruby

```ruby
class String
  def reverse_words
    self.split.reverse.join(" ")
  end
end

puts "hello world".reverse_words # Output: world hello
```

Cautions and Best Practices:

Careful Modification: Monkey patching can make code harder to understand and maintain, especially if done excessively.

Consider Alternatives: If possible, use inheritance, mixins, or method missing to extend functionality without directly modifying existing classes.

Testing Thoroughly: Thoroughly test any monkey patches to ensure they don't introduce unintended side effects.

Document Your Changes: Clearly document any monkey patches to explain their purpose and potential impact.

Use with Discernment: Monkey patching is a powerful tool, but it should be used judiciously and only when necessary.

When to Use Monkey Patching:

Temporary Fixes: For quick fixes or workarounds in specific contexts.

Customizing Third-Party Libraries: To adapt library behavior to your specific needs.

Testing and Debugging: To temporarily modify behavior for testing or debugging purposes.

Chapter 8

Building Web Applications with Ruby on Rails

8.1 Ruby on Rails: A Powerful Framework for Web Development

Ruby on Rails, often abbreviated as Rails, is a popular open-source web application framework written in the Ruby programming language. It follows the Model-View-Controller (MVC) architectural pattern, which[1] helps to organize web applications into three interconnected parts:

Model: Represents the data and business logic of the application.

View: Handles the presentation of the data to the user.

Controller: Manages the flow of the application, handling user requests and interacting with the model and view.

Key Features of Ruby on Rails:

Convention over Configuration: Rails follows a set of conventions, reducing the need for extensive configuration.

Rapid Development: Rails provides a high level of productivity, allowing developers to build web applications quickly.

Built-in Features: Rails includes features like scaffolding, database migrations, and asset pipelines, which streamline development.

Strong Community and Ecosystem: A large and active community provides extensive support, libraries, and frameworks.

Security: Rails has built-in security features to protect applications from common vulnerabilities.

Getting Started with Rails:

Install Ruby and Rails: Ensure you have Ruby and Rails installed on your system. You can use a package manager like `rbenv` or `rvm` to manage multiple Ruby versions.

Create a New Rails Application:

Bash

```
rails new my_app
```

Run the Development Server:

Bash

```
cd my_app
rails server
```

Explore the Generated Structure: Rails generates a well-organized project structure with directories for models, views, controllers, and other components.

Build Your Application: Start building your application by defining models, controllers, and views. Rails provides a set of conventions and generators to help you get started quickly.

Example:

Ruby

```ruby
# app/models/article.rb
class Article < ApplicationRecord
  validates :title, presence: true
end

# app/controllers/articles_controller.rb
class ArticlesController < ApplicationController
  def index
    @articles = Article.all
  end
end

# app/views/articles/index.html.erb
<h1>Articles</h1>
<ul>
  <% @articles.each do |article| %>
      <li><%= link_to article.title, article %></li>
  <% end %>
</ul>
```

Ruby on Rails is a powerful and flexible framework that can help you build robust and scalable web applications. By understanding its core concepts and conventions, you can leverage its capabilities to create amazing web experiences.

Would you like to delve deeper into a specific aspect of Rails, such as models, views, controllers, or database interactions?

8.2 Model-View-Controller (MVC) Architecture

Ruby on Rails, often abbreviated as Rails, is a popular open-source web application framework written in the Ruby programming language. It follows the Model-View-Controller (MVC) architectural pattern, which[1] helps to organize web applications into three interconnected parts:

Model: Represents the data and business logic of the application.

View: Handles the presentation of the data to the user.

Controller: Manages the flow of the application, handling user requests and interacting with the model and view.

Key Features of Ruby on Rails:

Convention over Configuration: Rails follows a set of conventions, reducing the need for extensive configuration.

Rapid Development: Rails provides a high level of productivity, allowing developers to build web applications quickly.

Built-in Features: Rails includes features like scaffolding, database migrations, and asset pipelines, which streamline development.

Strong Community and Ecosystem: A large and active community provides extensive support, libraries, and frameworks.

Security: Rails has built-in security features to protect applications from common vulnerabilities.

Getting Started with Rails:

Install Ruby and Rails: Ensure you have Ruby and Rails installed on your system. You can use a package manager like `rbenv` or `rvm` to manage multiple Ruby versions.

Create a New Rails Application:

Bash

```bash
rails new my_app
```

Run the Development Server:

Bash

```bash
cd my_app
rails server
```

Explore the Generated Structure: Rails generates a well-organized project structure with directories for models, views, controllers, and other components.

Build Your Application: Start building your application by defining models, controllers, and views. Rails provides a set of conventions and generators to help you get started quickly.

Example:

Ruby

```ruby
# app/models/article.rb
class Article < ApplicationRecord
  validates :title, presence: true
end

# app/controllers/articles_controller.rb
class ArticlesController < ApplicationController
```

```
  def index
    @articles = Article.all
  end
end

# app/views/articles/index.html.erb
<h1>Articles</h1>
<ul>
  <% @articles.each do |article| %>
      <li><%= link_to article.title, article
%></li>
  <% end %>
</ul>
```

Ruby on Rails is a powerful and flexible framework that can help you build robust and scalable web applications. By understanding its core concepts and conventions, you can leverage its capabilities to create amazing web experiences.

Would you like to delve deeper into a specific aspect of Rails, such as models, views, controllers, or database interactions?

8.3 Building a Simple Rails Application: A Step-by-Step Guide

Let's build a simple Rails application to manage a blog. We'll create models for `Post` and `Comment`, and set up basic CRUD (Create, Read, Update, Delete) operations.

1. Set Up a New Rails Application:

Bash

```
rails new blog_app
```

```
cd blog_app
```

2. Generate Models:

Bash

```
rails generate model Post title:string body:text
rails    generate    model    Comment    body:text
post:references
```

This will create two models: `Post` with `title` and `body` attributes, and `Comment` with `body` and a reference to a `Post`.

3. Set Up Migrations:

Bash

```
rails db:migrate
```

This will create the necessary database tables based on the defined models.

4. Create a Controller:

Bash

```
rails generate controller Posts index show new
create edit update destroy
```

This will generate a `PostsController` with actions for all CRUD operations.

5. Define Routes:

In `config/routes.rb`, you can define routes to map URLs to controller actions:

Ruby

```ruby
Rails.application.routes.draw do
  resources :posts do
    resources :comments, only: [:new, :create]
  end
  root 'posts#index'
end
```

6. Implement Controller Actions:

In `app/controllers/posts_controller.rb`, implement actions like:

Ruby

```ruby
def index
  @posts = Post.all
end

def show
  @post = Post.find(params[:id])
end

def new
  @post = Post.new
end
```

```
# ... other actions for create, edit, update, and
destroy
```

7. Create Views:

Index View: `app/views/posts/index.html.erb`

Show View: `app/views/posts/show.html.erb`

New View: `app/views/posts/new.html.erb`

Edit View: `app/views/posts/edit.html.erb`

You can use Rails' built-in form helpers to create HTML forms for creating and editing posts.

8. Start the Server:

Bash

```
rails server
```

Now, you can access your application in your browser at `http://localhost:3000`.

Additional Considerations:

Database Setup: Configure your database connection in `config/database.yml`.

User Authentication: Use a gem like Devise for user authentication and authorization.

Testing: Write tests for your controllers, models, and views using a testing framework like RSpec or Minitest.

Deployment: Deploy your application to a production server using a platform like Heroku, AWS, or DigitalOcean.

By following these steps and leveraging Rails' powerful features, you can quickly build robust and scalable web applications. Would you like to delve deeper into a specific aspect of Rails development, such as database interactions, testing, or deployment?

8.4 Routing, Controllers, and Views: The MVC Trio

In a Ruby on Rails application, the Model-View-Controller (MVC) architectural pattern plays a crucial role in organizing and structuring the code. Let's break down the three key components:

1. Routing

Routing defines how incoming HTTP requests are mapped to specific controller actions. It's configured in the `config/routes.rb` file.

Example:

Ruby

```ruby
Rails.application.routes.draw do
  root 'posts#index'
  resources :posts
end
```

This configuration defines:

The root path (/) maps to the `index` action of the `PostsController`.

The `resources :posts` line defines routes for all standard CRUD (Create, Read, Update, Delete) actions on the `PostsController`.

2. Controllers

Controllers handle incoming requests, process data, and render responses. They interact with models to retrieve and manipulate data.

Example:

Ruby

```ruby
class PostsController < ApplicationController
  def index
    @posts = Post.all
  end

  def show
    @post = Post.find(params[:id])
  end

  # ... other actions for create, update, destroy
end
```

In this example:

The `index` action fetches all posts from the database and assigns them to the `@posts` instance variable.

The `show` action fetches a specific post based on the `id` parameter and assigns it to the `@post` instance variable.

3. Views

Views are responsible for rendering the HTML that is sent to the user's browser. They use template languages like ERB to dynamically generate HTML.

Example:

HTML

```
<h1>Posts</h1>
<ul>
  <% @posts.each do |post| %>
    <li><%= link_to post.title, post %></li>
  <% end %>
</ul>
```

This view iterates over the `@posts` array and generates an unordered list of post titles, linking each title to the corresponding show page.

How They Work Together:

A user makes a request to a specific URL.

The router matches the URL to a controller action.

The controller action processes the request, fetches data from the model, and renders the appropriate view.

The rendered view is sent to the user's browser.

By understanding the roles of routing, controllers, and views, you can build well-structured and maintainable Rails applications.

Would you like to delve deeper into a specific aspect of Rails development, such as database interactions, testing, or deployment?

Chapter 9

Testing Your Ruby Applications

9.1 Introduction to Unit Testing

What is Unit Testing?

Unit testing is a software testing technique where individual units of code (functions, methods, or classes) are tested in isolation to ensure they work as expected. It's a crucial part of software development as it helps identify and fix bugs early in the development process.

Why Unit Testing is Important:

Early Bug Detection: By testing individual units, you can catch bugs early in the development cycle, making them easier and less costly to fix.

Improved Code Quality: Writing unit tests forces you to think about how your code will be used, leading to more robust and maintainable code.

Increased Confidence: Well-tested code gives you confidence in making changes, knowing that you can quickly identify and fix any unintended consequences.

Facilitates Refactoring: With a strong test suite, you can refactor your code with confidence, knowing that your changes won't break existing functionality.

How to Write Unit Tests:

Identify Units: Break down your code into testable units, such as functions, methods, or classes.

Write Test Cases: For each unit, write test cases that cover various input values and expected outputs.

Use a Testing Framework: A testing framework like RSpec or Minitest provides tools to organize and run tests.

Run Tests: Execute the tests to verify the correctness of your code.

Refactor and Retest: As you modify your code, update your tests to ensure they continue to pass.

Example using RSpec:

Ruby

```ruby
# lib/calculator.rb
class Calculator
  def add(x, y)
    x + y
  end
end


# spec/calculator_spec.rb
require 'calculator'

RSpec.describe Calculator do
  describe "#add" do
    it "adds two numbers" do
      calculator = Calculator.new
      expect(calculator.add(2, 3)).to eq(5)
    end
  end
end
```

Key Concepts in Unit Testing:

Test Cases: Individual test scenarios that verify specific behavior.

Test Suites: Collections of test cases that test a particular feature or module.

Test Doubles: Mock objects used to isolate units of code during testing.

Test-Driven Development (TDD): A development practice where tests are written before the actual code.

Test Coverage: A metric that measures the percentage of code covered by tests.

By incorporating unit testing into your development process, you can create higher-quality, more reliable, and maintainable software.

9.2 Writing Effective Tests with RSpec

RSpec is a popular testing framework for Ruby applications. It provides a domain-specific language (DSL) that makes writing tests more readable and expressive.

Basic RSpec Syntax:

Ruby

```ruby
RSpec.describe Calculator do
  describe "#add" do
    it "adds two numbers" do
      calculator = Calculator.new
      expect(calculator.add(2, 3)).to eq(5)
    end
  end
end
```

Key RSpec Matchers:

`expect(value).to eq(expected_value)`: Checks equality.

`expect(value).to be_truthy`: Checks if the value is truthy.

`expect(value).to be_falsey`: Checks if the value is falsy.

`expect(value).to be_nil`: Checks if the value is nil.

`expect(value).to be > 5`: Checks if the value is greater than 5.

`expect { block }.to raise_error(ErrorClass)`: Checks if a block raises a specific error.

Organizing Tests:

Describe Blocks: Define the context of a test, such as a class or module.

It Blocks: Specify individual test cases within a describe block.

Before and After Hooks: Execute code before or after each test or test suite.

Shared Examples: Reuse common test scenarios across multiple test suites.

Example with Before and After Hooks:

Ruby

```
RSpec.describe "Database operations" do
```

```ruby
before(:each) do
  # Setup database connection
end

after(:each) do
  # Clean up database
end

# ... test cases ...
end
```

Testing Controllers:

RSpec can also be used to test Rails controllers. You can test controller actions, responses, and redirects.

Ruby

```ruby
RSpec.describe PostsController, type: :controller do
  describe "GET #index" do
    it "returns a success response" do
      get :index

                              expect(response).to
have_http_status(:success)
    end
  end
end
```

Best Practices:

Write Clear and Concise Tests: Make your tests easy to read and understand.

Test Edge Cases: Consider boundary conditions and unexpected inputs.

Use Test Doubles: Isolate units of code with mocks and stubs to focus on specific behaviors.

Aim for High Test Coverage: Strive to cover as much of your code as possible with tests.

Refactor Your Tests: Keep your tests organized and maintainable.

By following these guidelines and leveraging RSpec's powerful features, you can write effective and reliable tests for your Ruby applications.

9.3 Test-Driven Development (TDD)

Test-Driven Development (TDD) is a software development approach where you write tests before writing the actual code. This approach promotes writing clean, well-tested code and helps catch bugs early in the development process.

TDD Cycle:

Write a Failing Test: Start by writing a test that fails because the code it's testing doesn't exist yet.

Write the Minimum Code: Write just enough code to make the test pass.

Refactor: Improve the code's design and readability without changing its behavior.

Repeat: Write the next test, and repeat the cycle.

Benefits of TDD:

Improved Code Quality: Writing tests forces you to think about the code's design and potential edge cases.

Early Bug Detection: By testing early and often, you can identify and fix bugs before they become more serious.

Increased Confidence: A solid test suite gives you confidence to make changes to your code.

Better Documentation: Tests serve as living documentation of your code's behavior.

Example:

Let's say we want to create a simple `Calculator` class with an `add` method.

Write the Failing Test:

Ruby

```ruby
require 'rspec'
require 'calculator'

RSpec.describe Calculator do
  describe "#add" do
    it "adds two numbers" do
      calculator = Calculator.new
      expect(calculator.add(2, 3)).to eq(5)
    end
  end
end
```

Write the Minimum Code:

Ruby

```ruby
class Calculator
  def add(x, y)
    x + y
```

```
    end
end
```

Refactor:

In this simple example, there's no need for refactoring. However, for more complex scenarios, you might refactor to improve code readability or performance.

Repeat:

Write more tests to cover different scenarios, such as negative numbers, zero, or floating-point numbers.

Key Takeaways:

Start Small: Begin with simple tests and gradually increase complexity.

Focus on One Test at a Time: Don't try to write all tests upfront.

Write Readable Tests: Use clear and concise language.

Use Test Doubles: Isolate units of code with mocks and stubs.

Don't Over-Test: Test the important parts of your code, but avoid excessive testing.

By following TDD principles, you can write high-quality, maintainable, and reliable Ruby code.

Chapter 10

Advanced Ruby Topics

10.1 Blocks and Iterators in Ruby

Blocks and iterators are powerful constructs in Ruby that allow you to iterate over collections, perform operations on each element, and create more concise and expressive code.

Blocks

A block is a piece of code enclosed in curly braces `{}` or the `do...end` keyword. It can be passed to methods as an argument.

Example:

Ruby

```ruby
[1, 2, 3].each { |number| puts number }
```

In this example, the block `{|number| puts number}` is passed to the `each` method. The block is executed for each element in the array, and the `number` variable holds the current element.

Iterators

Iterators are methods that allow you to iterate over collections and perform operations on each element. Common iterators in Ruby include:

`each`: Iterates over each element in a collection.

`map`: Creates a new array by transforming each element.

`select`: Creates a new array with elements that meet a certain condition.

`reduce`: Combines all elements into a single value.

`inject`: Similar to `reduce`, but with an initial value.

Example:

Ruby

```
numbers = [1, 2, 3, 4, 5]

# Using `each`
numbers.each { |number| puts number * 2 }

# Using `map`
doubled_numbers = numbers.map { |number| number *
2 }
puts doubled_numbers

# Using `select`
even_numbers    =    numbers.select    {    |number|
number.even? }
puts even_numbers

# Using `reduce`
sum = numbers.reduce { |sum, number| sum + number
}
puts sum
```

Yield Keyword

The `yield` keyword is used to pass control to a block within a method.

Example:

Ruby

```
def my_method
  yield 10
  yield 20
end

my_method { |number| puts number * 2 }
```

Key Points:

Blocks are often used with iterators to perform operations on each element of a collection.

The `yield` keyword can be used to pass control to a block within a method.

By mastering blocks and iterators, you can write more concise and expressive Ruby code.

By understanding blocks and iterators, you can write more elegant and efficient Ruby code.

10.2 Functional Programming with Ruby

Functional programming is a programming paradigm that emphasizes the use of pure functions, immutability, and higher-order functions.[1] While Ruby is primarily an object-oriented language, it supports functional programming concepts.

Pure Functions

A pure function is a function that:

Has no side effects: It doesn't modify any external state.

Is deterministic: Given the same input, it always returns the same output.

Example:

Ruby

```ruby
def add(x, y)
  x + y
end
```

Immutability

In functional programming, data is immutable, meaning it cannot be changed after it's created. Ruby supports immutability through techniques like creating new objects instead of modifying existing ones.

Example:

Ruby

```ruby
def increment(number)
  number + 1
end

number = 5
new_number = increment(number)
```

Higher-Order Functions

Higher-order functions are functions that can take other functions as arguments or return functions as results.[2]

Example:

Ruby

```ruby
def apply_function(number, function)
  function.call(number)
end

def square(x)
  x * x
end

result = apply_function(5, method(:square))
```

Functional Programming Techniques in Ruby

Using `map`, `reduce`, **and** `filter`: These methods allow you to transform, reduce, and filter collections in a functional style.

Using `inject`: This method is similar to `reduce`, but it takes an initial value.

Using `each_with_index`: This method iterates over a collection and yields each element along with its index.

Using `lazy`: This method creates lazy enumerators, which delay calculations until they are needed.

Example:

Ruby

```ruby
numbers = [1, 2, 3, 4, 5]

# Using `map`
squares = numbers.map { |number| number * number
}

# Using `select`
even_numbers  =  numbers.select  {  |number|
number.even? }

# Using `reduce`
sum = numbers.reduce(0) { |sum, number| sum +
number }
```

By embracing functional programming principles, you can write more concise, readable, and maintainable Ruby code.

10.3 Concurrent and Parallel Programming in Ruby

Concurrent and parallel programming are techniques used to improve the performance and responsiveness of applications. While both involve executing multiple tasks simultaneously, they have distinct approaches.

Concurrent Programming

Concurrent programming involves executing multiple tasks within a single process. This is often achieved using techniques like threads or asynchronous programming.

Threads: Threads are lightweight processes that share the same memory space. Ruby provides the `Thread` class for creating and managing threads.

Ruby

```ruby
Thread.new { puts "Hello from a thread!" }.join
```

Asynchronous Programming: Asynchronous programming involves non-blocking operations, allowing the program to handle multiple tasks without waiting for each task to complete. Ruby's `Async` library is a popular choice for asynchronous programming.

Parallel Programming

Parallel programming involves executing multiple tasks across multiple processors or cores. This is typically achieved using processes or multiple threads.

Processes: Processes are independent programs that have their own memory space. Ruby's `Process.fork` method can be used to create new processes.

Multiple Threads: In some cases, using multiple threads can improve performance, especially for CPU-bound tasks.

Key Considerations:

Shared State: When working with shared state (e.g., variables, objects), careful synchronization is necessary to avoid race conditions and data corruption.

Concurrency Model: Choose the appropriate concurrency model (threads, processes, or asynchronous programming) based on the specific requirements of your application.

Performance Bottlenecks: Identify and optimize performance bottlenecks to maximize the benefits of concurrent and parallel programming.

Testing: Thoroughly test concurrent and parallel code to ensure correctness and reliability.

Example: Concurrent Web Server

Ruby

```ruby
require 'socket'

server = TCPServer.open(2000)

loop do
  Thread.start(server.accept) do |client|
    client.puts "Hello from the server!"
    client.close
  end
end
```

This simple web server handles incoming connections concurrently, creating a new thread for each client.

In Conclusion

Concurrent and parallel programming can significantly improve the performance and responsiveness of Ruby applications. However, it's important to use these techniques judiciously and to be aware of the potential challenges, such as synchronization and performance overhead.

10.4 Deploying Ruby Applications

Deploying a Ruby on Rails application involves making your application accessible to the public. Here are some common deployment strategies:

Platform as a Service (PaaS):

Heroku: A popular platform that simplifies deployment and scaling.

AWS Elastic Beanstalk: A fully managed platform that handles infrastructure and deployment.

Google App Engine: A platform for building scalable web applications and mobile backends.

Advantages:

Easy to set up and manage.

Automatic scaling.

Built-in security features.

Infrastructure as a Service (IaaS):

AWS: Offers a wide range of services, including EC2 instances, S3 storage, and RDS databases.

DigitalOcean: A cloud platform that provides virtual machines, storage, and networking.

Google Cloud Platform (GCP): Offers a suite of cloud computing services, including Compute Engine, App Engine, and Cloud Storage.

Advantages:

Greater flexibility and control.

Cost-effective for large-scale applications.

Deployment Steps:

Prepare Your Application:

Ensure your application is in a deployable state.

Configure your database settings for the production environment.

Set up environment variables for sensitive information.

Choose a Deployment Strategy:

Select a deployment method, such as Git deployment or Capistrano.

Configure Your Deployment Server:

Set up a server with the necessary software (Ruby, Rails, database, web server).

Configure the server's firewall to allow incoming traffic.

Deploy Your Application:

Use a deployment tool to transfer your application code to the server.

Configure your web server (e.g., Nginx, Apache) to serve your application.

Configure Your Database:

Set up your database (e.g., PostgreSQL, MySQL) and configure it to work with your application.

Set Up a Process Manager:

Use a process manager like `Procfile` or `Passenger` to manage your application's processes.

Configure a Reverse Proxy:

Set up a reverse proxy (e.g., Nginx) to handle incoming traffic and distribute it to your application servers.

Additional Considerations:

Security: Implement security measures like HTTPS, strong passwords, and regular security updates.

Monitoring: Use tools like New Relic or Datadog to monitor your application's performance and health.

Logging: Set up logging to track errors and debug issues.

Backup and Recovery: Implement a backup strategy to protect your data.

By following these steps and considering the specific requirements of your application, you can successfully deploy your Ruby on Rails application to production.

www.ingramcontent.com/pod-product-compliance
Lightning Source LLC
LaVergne TN
LVHW012337060326
832902LV00012B/1917